CONTENTS

BIBLIOGRAPHY

Shaw, Bernard. *The Admirable Bashville; or, Constancy Unrewarded.* Brentano's, 1909, New York.

Shaw, Bernard. *The Doctor's Dilemma.* Brentano's, 1909, New York.

Shaw, Bernard. (Includes: *Major Barbara, How He Lied to Her Husband.*) Brentano's, 1907, New York.

Shaw, Bernard. *Man and Superman.* Brentano's, 1909, New York.

Shaw, Bernard. *Plays: Pleasant and Unpleasant, Vol. 1.* (Includes: *Widower's Houses, The Philanderer, Mrs. Warren's Profession.*) Brentano's, 1907, New York.

Shaw, Bernard. *Plays: Pleasant and Unpleasant, Vol. 2.* (Includes: *You Never Can Tell, Arms and the Man, Candida, The Man of Destiny.*) Herbert S. Stone & Company, 1904, Chicago.

Shaw, Bernard. *Three Plays for Puritans.* (Includes: *Caesar and Cleopatra, Captain Brassbound's Conversion.*) Brentano's, 1906, New York.

WOMEN

The Dark Lady of the Sonnets

The Lady (Queen Elizabeth I) comes upon the Man Shakespear [sic], saying the lines which Shakespear later stole and used in his plays.

THE LADY

(*Rubbing her hands as if washing them.*) Out, damned spot. You will mar all with these cosmetics. God made you one face; and you make yourself another. Think of your grave, woman, not ever of being beautiful. All the perfumes of Arabia will not whiten this Tudor hand.

Mary! Mary! Who would have thought that woman to have had so much blood in her! Is it my fault that my counsellors put deeds of blood on me? Fie! If you were woman you would have more wit than to stain the floor so foully. Hold not up her head so: the hair is false. I tell you yet again, Mary's buried: she cannot come out of the grave. I hear her not: these cats that dare jump into thrones though they be fit only for men's laps must be put away. What's done cannot be undone. Out, I say. Fie! a queen, and freckled!

You Never Can Tell, Act I

Mrs. Clandon discourses upon the need for equality in a family.

MRS. CLANDON

(*Rising, the placidity of her age broken up; and a curious excitement, dignified but dogged, ladylike, implacable.*) Phil: take care. Remember what I have always taught you. There are two sorts of family life, Phil; and your experience of human nature only extends, so far, to one of them. (*Rhetorically.*) The sort you know is based on mutual respect, or recognition of the right of every member of the household to independence and privacy (*With the emphasis on "privacy."*) in their personal concerns. And because you have always enjoyed that, it seems such a matter of course to you that you don't value it.

But (*With biting acrimony.*) there is another sort of family life; a life in which husbands open their wives' letters, and call on them to accounts for every farthing of their expenditure and every moment of their time; in which women do the same to their children; in which no room is private and no hour sacred; in which duty, obedience, affection, home, morality, and religion are detestable tyrannies, and life is a vulgar round of punishments and lies, coercion and rebellion, jealousy, suspicion, recrimination—Oh! I cannot describe it to you: fortunately for you, you know nothing about it.
(*She sits, panting.*)

Arms and the Man, Act I

Raina reflects on her hero-worship of Sergius to her mother, Catherine.

RAINA

Our ideas of what Sergius would do—our patriotism —our heroic ideals. I sometimes used to doubt whether they were anything but dreams. When I buckled on Sergius' sword he looked so noble: it was treason to think of disillusion or humiliation or failure. And yet— yet—(*Quickly.*) Promise me you'll never tell him. (*Pause.*) Well, it came into my head just as he was holding me in his arms and looking into my eyes, that perhaps we only had our heroic ideas because we are so fond of reading Byron and Pushkin, and because we were so delighted with the opera that season in Bucharest. Real life is so seldom like that—indeed never, as far as I knew it then. (*Remorsefully.*) Only think, mother, I doubted him: I wondered whether all his heroic qualities and his soldiership might not prove mere imagination when he went into real battle. I had an uneasy fear that he might cut a poor figure there beside all those clever Russian officers. (*Pause.*) Yes, I was only a prosaic little coward. Oh, to think that it was all true —that Sergius is just as splendid and noble as he looks—that the world is really a glorious world for women who can see its glory and men who can act its romance! What happiness! What unspeakable fulfillment! Ah!

Candida, Act III

While attempting to talk Marchbanks out of his infatuation with her, Candida describes her relationship with her husband Morell.

CANDIDA

(*Smiling a little.*) Let us sit and talk comfortable over it like three friends. (*To Morell.*) Sit down, dear. Bring me that chair, Eugene. (*He fetches the chair for her, she sits. When they are all settled she begins, throwing a spell of quietness on them by her calm, sane, tender tone.*) You remember what you told me about yourself, Eugene: how nobody has cared for you since your old nurse died: how those clever, fashionable sisters and successful brothers of yours were your mother's and father's pets: how miserable you were at Eton: how your father is trying to starve you into returning to Oxford: how you have had to live without comfort or welcome or refuge, always lonely, and nearly always disliked and misunderstood, poor boy!

Now I want you to look at this other boy here—my boy—spoiled from the cradle. We go once a fortnight to see his parents. You should come with us, Eugene, and see the pictures of the hero of that household. James as a baby! the most wonderful of all babies. James holding his first school prize, won at the ripe age of eight! James as the captain of his eleven! James in his first frock coat! James under all sorts of glorious circumstances! You know how strong he is (I hope he didn't hurt you)—how clever he is—how happy! (*With deepening gravity.*) Ask James' mother and his three sisters what it cost to save James the trouble of doing anything but be strong and clever and happy. Ask me what it costs to be James' mother and three sisters and wife and mother to his three children all at once. Ask Prossy and Maria how troublesome the house is even when we have no visitors to help us to slice the onions. Ask the tradesmen who want to worry James and spoil his beautiful sermons who it is that puts them off. When there is money to give, he gives it: when there is money to refuse, I refuse it. I build a castle of comfort and indulgence and love for him, and stand sentinel always to keep little vulgar cares out. I make him master here, though he does not know it, and could not tell you a moment ago how it came to be so. (*With sweet irony.*) And when he thought I might go away with you, his only anxiety was what should become of me! And to tempt me to stay he offered me his strength for my defence, his industry for my livelihood, his position for my dignity, his— (*Relenting.*) Ah, I am mixing up your beautiful sentences and spoiling them, am I not, darling?

The Philanderer, Act I

Julia, forsaken by Leonard Charteris for Grace, pleads her case to him.

JULIA

(*Vehemently and movingly; for she is now sincere.*) No. You made me pay dearly for every moment of happiness. You revenged yourself on me for the humiliation of being the slave of your passion for me. I was never sure of you for a moment. I trembled whenever a letter came from you, lest it should contain some stab for me. I dreaded your visits almost as much as I longed for them. I was your plaything, not your companion. Oh, there was such suffering in my happiness that I hardly knew joy from pain. (*She buries her face in her hands and turns from him.*) Better for me I had never met you!

But why? We could be so happy. You love me—I know you love me—I can feel it. You say "My dear" to me: you have said it several times this evening. I know I have been wicked, odious, bad. I say nothing in defence of myself. But don't be hard on me. I was distracted by the thought of losing you. I can't face life without you Leonard. I was happy when I met you: I had never loved anyone; and if you had only let me alone I could have gone on contentedly by myself. But I can't now. I must have you with me. Don't cast me off without a thought of all I have at stake. I could be a friend to you if you would only let me—if you would only tell me your plans—give me a share in your work—treat me as something more than the amusement of an idle hour.

Oh, Leonard, Leonard, you've never given me a chance: indeed you haven't. I'll take pains; I'll read; I'll try to think; I'll conquer my jealousy; I'll— (*She breaks down.*) Oh, I'm mad: I'm mad: you'll kill me if you desert me.

The test of a man's or woman's breeding is how they behave in a quarrel.
G.B.S., *The Philanderer*

Man and Superman, Act III

In the "Don Juan In Hell" scene, Dona Ana (Ann Whitefield) takes a stand for the rights of women.

ANA

You are talking to a woman of seventy-seven now. If you had had a chance, you would have run away from me too if I had let you. You would not have found it so easy with me as with some of the others. If men will not be faithful to their home and their duties, they must be made be. I daresay you all want to marry lovely incarnations of music and painting and poetry. Well, you can't have them, because they don't exist. If flesh and blood is not good enough for you you must go without: that's all. Women have to put up with flesh-and-blood husbands—and little enough of that too, sometimes; and you will have to put up with flesh-and-blood wives. (*The Devil looks dubious. The statue makes a wry face.*) I see you don't like that, any of you, but it's true, for all that; so if you don't like it you can lump it.

> *Silence is the most perfect expression of scorn.*
> G.B.S., *Back to Methuselah*

The Admirable Bashville; or, Constancy Unrewarded, Act I

In this opening speech of the play Lydia is yearning for love.

LYDIA

Ye leafy breasts and warm protecting wings
O mother trees that hatch our tender souls,
And from the well of nature in our hearts
Thaw the intolerable inch of ice
That bears the weight of all the stamping world,
Hear ye me sing of solitude that I,
Lydia Carew, the owner of these lands,
Albeit most rich, most learned, and most wise,
And yet most lonely. What are riches worth
When wisdom with them comes to shew the
  purse bearer
That life remains unpurchasable? Learning
Learns but one lesson: doubt! To excel all
Is, to be lonely. Oh, ye busy birds,
Engrossed with real needs, ye shameless trees
With arms outstretched in welcome of the sun,
Your minds, bent singly to enlarge your lives,
Have given you wings and raised your delicate heads
High heavens above us crawlers.

Lo, the leaves
That hide my drooping boughs! Mock me—poor maid!—Deride
with joyous comfortable chatter
These stolen feathers. Laugh at me, the clothed one.
Laugh at the mind fed on foul air and books.

Books! Art! And Culture! Oh, I shall go mad.
Give me a mate that never heard of these,
A sylvan god, tree born in heart and sap;
Or else, eternal maidhood be my hap.

Physically there is nothing to distinguish human society from the farm-yard except that children are more troublesome and costly than chickens and women are not so completely enslaved as farm stock.
G.B.S., *Getting Married,* Preface

The Admirable Bashville; or, Constancy Unrewarded, Act II

Adelaide has just discovered that her son is a boxer.

ADELAIDE

A ribald peer,
Lord Worthington by name, this morning came
With honeyed words beseeching me to mount
His four-in-hand, and to the country hie
To see some English sport. Being by nature
Frank as a child, I fell into the snare,
But took so long to dress that the design
Failed of its full effect; for not until
The final round we reached the horrid scene.
Be silent all; for now I do approach
My tragedy's catastrophe. Know, then,
That Heaven did bless me with only one son,
A boy devoted to his doting mother—
Ten years ago my darling disappeared
(Ten dreary twelvemonths of continuous tears,
Tears that have left me prematurely aged;
For I am younger far than I appear).
Judge of my anguish when I today saw
Stripped to the waist, and fighting like a demon
With one who, whatsoe'er his humble virtues,
Was clearly not a gentleman, my son!

Major Barbara, Act III

Despite her dedication to her work with the Salvation Army, Barbara is convinced by Undershaft's tirade on the hypocrisy of society, and approves of Cusins' decision to become Undershaft's heir to the munitions factory.

BARBARA

There is no wicked side; life is all one. And I never wanted to shirk my share in whatever evil must be endured, whether it be sin of suffering. I wish I could cure you of middle-class ideas, Dolly.

That is why I have no class, Dolly: I come straight out of the heart of the whole people. If I were middle-class I should turn my back on my father's business; and we should both live in an artistic drawing room, with you reading the reviews in one corner, and I in the other at the piano, playing Shumann: both very superior persons, and neither of us a bit of use. Sooner than that, I would sweep out the guncotton shed, or be one of Bodger's barmaids. Do you know what would have happened if you had refused papa's offer?

I should have given you up and married the man who accepted it. After all, my dear old mother has more sense than any of you. I felt like her when I saw this place—felt that I must have it—that never, never, never could I let it go; only she thought it was the houses and the kitchen ranges and the linen and china, when it was really all the human souls to be saved: not weak souls in starved bodies, sobbing with gratitude for a scrap of bread and treacle, but fullfed, quarrelsome, snobbish, uppish creatures, all standing on their little rights and dignities, and thinking that my father ought to be greatly obliged to them for making so much money for him—and so he ought. That is where salvation is really wanted. My father shall never throw it in my teeth again that my converts were bribed with bread. I have got rid of the bribe of heaven. Let God's work be done for its own sake: the work he had to create us to do because it cannot be done except by living men and women. When I die, let him be in my debt, not I in his; and let me forgive him as becomes a woman of my rank.

> *With the single exception of Homer, there is no eminent writer, not even Sir Walter Scott, whom I can despise so entirely as I despise Shakespeare when I measure my mind against his. . . . It would positively be a relief to me to dig him up and throw stones at him.*
> G.B.S., *Dramatic Opinions and Essays, Volume 2*

The Doctor's Dilemma, Act III

In her ongoing effort to seek medical care for Louis Dubedat, Jennifer Dubedat is attempting to plead her husband's case as a human being to Sir Colenso Ridgeon.

MRS. DUBEDAT

He is perhaps sometimes weak about women, because they adore him so, and are always laying traps for him. And of course when he says he doesn't believe in morality, ordinary pious people think he must be wicked. You can understand, can't you, how all this starts a great deal of gossip about him, and gets repeated until even good friends get set against him?

Oh, if you only knew the other side of him as I do! I had a great many dreams; but at last they all came to one dream. I could do nothing myself; but I had a little property and I could help with it. I had even a little beauty; don't think me vain for knowing it. I knew that men of genius always had a terrible struggle with poverty and neglect at first. My dream was to save one of them from that, and bring some charm and happiness into his life. I prayed heaven to send me one. I firmly believe Louis was guided to me in answer to my prayer. He was no more like the other men I had met than the Thames Embankment is like our Cornish coasts. He saw everything I saw, and drew it from me. He understood everything. He came to me like a child. Only fancy, doctor: He never even wanted to marry me: He never thought of the things other men think of! I had to propose it myself. Then he said he had no money. When I told him I had some, he said "Oh, all right" just like a boy. He is still like that, quite unspoiled, a man in his thoughts, a great poet and artist in his dreams, and a child in his ways. I gave him myself and all that I had that he might grow to his full height with plenty of sunshine. If I lost faith in him, it would mean the wreck and failure of my life. I should go back to Cornwall and die. I could shew you the very cliff I should jump off. You must cure him: You must make him quite well again for me. I know that you can do it and that nobody else can. I implore you not to refuse what I am going to ask you to do. Take Louis yourself; and let Sir Ralph cure Dr. Blenkinsop.

> *The worst sin towards our fellow creatures is not to hate them, but to be indifferent to them: that's the essence of inhumanity.*
>
> G.B.S., *The Devil's Disciple*

Widower's Houses, Act III

Blanche (Sartorius' daughter), after having refused the attentions of Trench, due to the fact that he will not accept money from Sartorius, works herself around to making up with him.

BLANCHE

(*Shrewishly.*) Well? So you have come back here. You have had the meanness to come into this house again. (*He flushes and retreats a step. She follows him remorselessly.*) What a poor-spirited creature you must be! Why don't you go! (*He attempts to leave but she blocks his exit.*) I don't want you to stay. (*For a moment they stand facing each other, quite close, she provocative, taunting, half defying, half inviting him to advance, in a flush of undisguised animal excitement. It suddenly occurs to him that all this is very erotic—that she is making love to him. With a heavy assumption of indifference he returns directly to his chair, plants himself in it with his arms folded. She comes down the room after him.*) But I forgot: You have found that there is some money to be made here. Lickcheese told you. You, who were so disinterested, so independent, that you could not accept anything from my father! (*At the end of each sentence she waits to see what execution she has done.*) I suppose that you will try to persuade me that you have come down here on a great philanthropic enterprise—to befriend the poor by having those houses rebuilt, eh? (*He maintains his attitude of indifference.*) Yes, when my father makes you do it. And when Lickcheese has discovered some way of making it profitable. Oh, I know papa; and I know you. And for the sake of that, you come back here—into the house where you were refused—ordered out. (*Trench's face darkens: her eyes gleam as she see this.*) Aha! You remember that. You know it is true, you cannot deny it. (*She sits, softens her tone, affecting pity.*) Ah, let me tell you that you cut a poor figure, a very, very poor figure, Harry. And you, too, a gentleman!—so highly connected!—with such distinguished relations!—so particular as to where your money comes from!—I wonder at you. I really wonder at you. I should have thought that if your family brought you nothing else, it might at least have brought you some sense of personal dignity. Perhaps you think you look dignified at present, eh? (*No reply.*) Well, I can assure you that you don't: You look most ridiculous—as foolish as a man could look—you don't know what to say; and you don't know what to do. But after all, I really don't see what anyone could say in defence of such conduct. (*He looks straight ahead, purses his lips as if whistling. This annoys her and she becomes affectedly polite.*) I am afraid I am in your way, Dr.Trench. (*She rises.*) I shall not intrude on you any longer. You seem so perfectly at home that I need make no apology for leaving you to yourself. (*She feigns going to the door; but he does not budge; she returns and comes behind his chair.*) Harry, I want you to answer me a question. (*Earnestly, stooping over him.*) Look me in the face. (*No reply.*) Do you hear? (*Putting her hand on his shoulder.*) Look—me—

in—the—face.(*He still stares straight ahead. She suddenly kneels down beside him with her breast against his right shoulder; taking his face in her hands, and twisting it sharply towards her.*) Harry: What were you doing with my photograph just now, when you thought you were alone? (*He fights back a smile. She flings her arms around him, and crushes him in an ecstatic embrace. She speaks with great tenderness.*) How dare you touch anything belonging to me?

> *There are two tragedies in life. One is to lose your heart's desire.The other is to gain it.*
> G.B.S., *Man and Superman*

Mrs. Warren's Profession, Act II

Kitty Warren explains to her daughter, Vivie, the circumstances of her early life that led to her career in prostitution.

MRS. WARREN

D'you know what your gran'mother was? No, you don't. I do. She called herself a widow and had a fried-fish shop down by the mint, and kept herself and four daughters out of it. Two of us were sisters: that was me and Liz; and we were both good-looking and well made. I suppose our father was a well-fed man: Mother pretends he was a gentleman; but I don't know. The other two were only half sisters: undersized, ugly, starved looking, hard working, honest poor creatures: Liz and I would have half-murdered them if mother hadn't half-murdered us to keep our hands off them. They were the respectable ones. Well, what did they get by their respectability? I'll tell you. One of them worked in a white-lead factory twelve hours a day for nine shillings a week until she died of lead poisoning. She only expected to get her hands a little paralyzed; but she died. The other was always held up to us as a model because she married a government laborer in the Deptford victualling yard, and kept his room and the three children neat and tidy on eighteen shillings a week—until he took to drink. That was worth being respectable for, wasn't it?

We both went to a church school—that was part of the ladylike airs we gave ourselves to be superior to the children that knew nothing and went nowhere—and we stayed there until Liz went out one night and never came back. I know the schoolmistress thought I'd soon follow her example; for the clergyman was warning me that Lizzie'd end up jumping off the Waterloo Bridge. Poor fool: That was all he knew about it! But I was more afraid of the white-lead factory than I was of the river; and so would you have been in my place. That clergyman got me a situation as a scullery maid in a temperance restaurant where they sent out for anything you liked. Then I was waitress; and then I went to the bar at the Waterloo station: Fourteen hours a day serving drinks and washing glasses for four shillings a week and my board. That was considered a great promotion for me. Well, one cold, wretched night, when I was so tired I could hardly keep myself awake, who should come up for a half of Scotch but Lizzie, in a long fur cloak, elegant and comfortable, with a lot of sovereigns in her purse. No river for Liz, thank you! You remind me of Liz a little: She was a first-rate business woman—saved money from the beginning—never let herself look too much like what she was—never lost her head or threw away a chance. When she saw I'd grown up good-looking she said to me across the bar "What are you doing here, you little fool? Wearing out your health and your appearance for other people's profit!" Liz was saving money then to take a house for herself in Brussels; and she thought we two could save faster than one. So she lent me some money and gave me a start; and I saved steadily and first paid her back, and then went into business with her as a partner. Why shouldn't I have done it? The house in Brussels was real high class: a much better place for a woman to be in than the factory where Aunt Jane got poisoned. None of our girls were ever treated as I was treated in the scullery of that temperance place, or at the Waterloo bar, or a home. Would you have had me stay in them and become a worn out old drudge before I was forty?

> *This writing of plays is a great matter, forming as it does the minds and affections of men in such sort that whatsoever they see done in show on the stage, they will presently be doing in earnest in the world, which is but a larger stage.*
> G.B.S., *The Dark Lady of the Sonnets*

MEN

Man And Superman, Act I

John Tanner is attempting to expose the inconsistencies of Ann Whitefield's character. A young woman who is skilled in the art of manipulating others to her will.

TANNER

(*Working himself into a sociological rage.*) Oh, I protest against this vile abjection of youth to age! Look at fashionable society as you know it. What does it pretend to be? An exquisite dance of nymphs. What is it? A horrible procession of wretched girls, each in the claws of a cynical, cunning, avaricious, disillusioned, ignorantly experienced, foul-minded old woman whom she calls her mother, and whose duty is to corrupt her mind and sell her to the highest bidder. Why do these unhappy slaves marry anybody, however old and vile, sooner than not marry at all? Because marriage is their only means of escape from these decrepit fiends who hide their selfish ambitions, their jealous hatreds of the young rivals who have supplanted them, under the mask of maternal duty and family affection. Such things are abominable: the voice of nature proclaims for the daughter a father's care and for the son a mother's. The law for father and son and mother and daughter is not the law of love: It is the law of revolution, of emancipation, of final supersession of the old and worn-out by the young and capable. I tell you, the first duty of manhood and womanhood is a Declaration of Independence: The man who pleads his father's authority is no man: The woman who pleads her mother's authority is unfit to bear citizens to a free people.

Break your chains. Go your way according to your own conscience and not according to your mother's. Get your mind clean and vigorous; and learn to enjoy a fast ride in a motor car instead of seeing nothing in it but an excuse for a detestable intrigue. Come with me to Marseilles and across to Algiers and to Biskra, at sixty miles an hour. Come right down to the Cape if you like. That will be a Declaration of Independence with a vengeance. You can write a book about it afterwards. That will finish your mother and make a woman of you.

> *Alcohol is a necessary article. It enables Parliament to do things at eleven at night that no sane person would do at eleven in the morning.*
> G.B.S., *Major Barbara*

Man and Superman, Act I

John Tanner is telling Octavius, a self-proclaimed artist and sensitive human being, what the true characteristics of an artist are.

TANNER

The true artist will let his wife starve, his children go barefoot, his mother drudge for his living at seventy, sooner than work at anything but his art. To women he is half vivisector, half vampire. He gets into intimate relations with them to study them, to strip the mask of convention from them, to surprise their in-innermost secrets, knowing that they have the power to rouse his deepest creative energies, to rescue him from his cold reason, to make him see visions and dream dreams, to inspire him, as he calls it. He persuades women that they may do this for their own purpose whilst he really means them to do it for his. He steals the mother's milk and blackens it to make printer's ink to scoff at her and glorify ideal women with. He pretends to spare her the pangs of child-bearing so that he may have for himself the tenderness and fostering that belong of right to her children. Since marriage began, the great artist has been known as a bad husband. But he is worse: He is a child-robber, a blood-sucker, a hypocrite and a cheat. Perish the race and wither a thousand women if only the sacrifice of them enable him to act Hamlet better, to paint a finer picture, to write a deeper poem, a greater play, a profounder philosophy! For mark you, Tavy, the artist's work is to shew us ourselves as we really are. Our minds are nothing but this knowledge of ourselves; and he who adds a jot to such knowledge creates new mind as surely as any woman creates new men. In the rage of that creation he is as ruthless as the women, as dangerous to her as she to him, and as horribly fascinating. Of all human struggles there is none so treacherous and remorseless as the struggle between the artist man and the mother woman. Which shall use up the other? that is the issue between them. And it is all the deadlier because, in your romanticist cant, they love one another.

> *Give women the vote, and in five years there will be a crushing tax on bachelors.*
> G.B.S., *Man and Superman*

The Doctor's Dilemma, Act I

Ridgeon describes the discovery that got him knighted.

RIDGEON

No: It's not gammon. What it comes to in practice is this. The phagocytes won't eat the microbes unless the microbes are nicely buttered for them. Well, the patient manufactures the butter for himself all right; but my discovery is that the manufacture of that butter, which I call opsonin, goes on in the system by ups and downs—Nature being always rhythmical, you know—and that what the inoculation does is to stimulate the ups and downs, as the case may be. If we had inoculated Jane Marsh when her butter factory was on the up-grade, we should have cured her arm. But we got in on the down-grade and lost her arm for her. I call the up-grade the positive phase and the down-grade the negative phase. Everything depends on your inoculating at the right moment. Inoculate when the patient is in the negative phase and you kill: Inoculate when the patient is in the positive phase and you cure. Send a drop of the patient's blood to the laboratory at St. Anne's, and in fifteen minutes I'll give you his opsonin index in figures. If the figure is one, inoculate and cure: If it's under point eight, inoculate and kill. That's my discovery: The most important that has been made since Harvey discovered the circulation of the blood. My tuberculosis patients don't die now.

Captain Brassbound's Conversion, Act III

Captain Brassbound, who has scorned love in the past, proposes marriage to Lady Cicely.

BRASSBOUND

I want a commander. Don't undervalue me: I am a good man when I have a good leader. I have courage: I have determination: I'm not a drinker: I can command a schooner and a shore party if I can't command a ship or an army. When work is put upon me, I turn neither to save my life nor to fill my pocket. Gordon trusted me: and he never regretted it. If you trust me, you shant regret it. All the same, there's something wanting in me: I suppose I'm stupid. Since you saw me for the first time in that garden, you've heard me say nothing clever. And I've heard you say nothing that didn't make me laugh, or make me feel friendly, as well as telling me what to think and what to do. That's what I mean by real cleverness. Well, I haven't got it.

I can give an order when I know what order to give. I can make men obey it, willing or unwilling. But I'm stupid, I tell you: Stupid. When there's no Gordon to command me, I can't think of what to do. Left to myself, I've become half a brigand. I can kick that little gutterscrub Drinkwater; but I find myself doing what he puts into my head because I can't think of anything else. When you came, I took your orders as naturally as Gordon's, though I little thought my next commander would be a woman. I want to take service under you. And there is no way in which that can be done except marrying you. Will you let me do it?

> *Heaven, as conventionally conceived, is a place so inane, so dull, so useless, so miserable, that nobody has ever ventured to describe a whole day in heaven, though plenty of people have described a day at the seaside.*
> G.B.S., *Misalliance,* Preface

You Never Can Tell, Act II

A waiter gives a truer philosophy of life than any of the upper classes is capable of giving.

WAITER

(*Philosophically.*) Well, sir, you never can tell. That's the principle in life with me, sir, if you'll excuse my having such a thing, sir. (*Artfully loosing the philosopher for a moment.*) Perhaps you haven't noticed that you hadn't touched that seltzer and Irish, sir, when the party broke up. (*Sets a tumbler before Crampton.*) Yes, sir, you never can tell. There was my son, sir! whoever thought that he would rise to wear a silk gown, sir? What a lesson, sir. (*Artfully digressing.*) A lump of sugar, sir, will take the flatness out of the seltzer without noticeably sweetening the drink, sir. Allow me, sir. (*Places the tumbler.*) But as I say to him, where's the difference after all? If I must put on a dress coat to show what I am, sir, he must put on a wig and gown to show what he is. If my income is mostly tips, and there's a pretence that I don't get them, why, his income is mostly fees, sir; and I understand that there's a pretence that he don't get them! If he likes society, and if his profession brings him into contact with all ranks, so does mine too, sir. If it's a little against a barrister to have a waiter for his father, sir, it's a little against a waiter to have a barrister for a son; many people consider it a great liberty, sir, I assure you, sir. Can I get you anything else, sir?

You Never Can Tell, Act III

In pleading his case for loving Gloria, Valentine discourses upon the battle between the sexes.

VALENTINE

During the whole century, my dear Mrs. Clandon, the progress of artillery has been a duel between the maker of cannons and the maker of armor plates to keep the cannon balls out. You build a ship proof against the best gun known: Somebody makes a better gun and sinks your ship. You build a heavier ship, proof against that gun: Somebody makes a heavier gun and sinks you again. And so on. Well, the duel of sex is just like that. Now what happens in the duel of sex? The old fashioned mother received an old fashioned education to protect her against the wiles of man. Well, you know the result: The old fashioned man got round her. The old fashioned woman resolved to protect her daughter more effectually—to find some armor too strong for the old fashioned man. So she gave her daughter a scientific education—your plan. That was a corker for the old fashioned man: He said it wasn't fair—unwomanly and all the rest of it. But that didn't do him any good. So he had to give up his old fashioned plan of attack—you know—going down on his knees and swearing to love, honor, and obey, and so on.

Well, what did the man do? Just what the artillery man does—went one better than the woman—educated himself scientifically and beat her at the game just as he had beaten her at the old game. I learnt how to circumvent the Women's Rights woman before I was twenty-three: it's all been found out long ago. You see, my methods are thoroughly modern.

QUOTATIONS ABOUT G.B. SHAW

He writes like a Pakistani who has learned English when he was twelve years old in order to become a chartered accountant.
John Osborne, British dramatist

Shaw's works make me admire the magnificent tolerance and broadmindedness of the English.
James Joyce

The Admirable Bashville; or, Constancy Unrewarded, Act II

The servant, Bashville, is reading a newspaper account of a boxing match, in which Cashel Byron (the man Lydia loves) has participated.

BASHVILLE

(*Reading.*) "At noon today, unknown to
the police,
Within a thousand miles of Wormwood Scrubbs,
The Australian Champion and his challenger,
The Flying Dutchman, formerly engaged
I' the mercantile marine, fought to a finish.
Lord Worthington, the well-known sporting peer,
Was early on the scene."
"The bold Ned Skene revisited the ropes
To hold the bottle for his quondam novice;
Whilst in the seaman's corner were assembled
Professor Palmer and the Chelsea Snob.
Mellish, whose epigastrium has been hurt,
Tis said, by accident at Wiltstoken,
Looked none the worse in the Australian's corner.
The Flying Dutchman wore the Union Jack:
His colors freely sold amid the crowd;
But Cashel's well-known spot of white on blue—
Was fairly rushed for. Time was called at twelve,
When, with a smile of confidence upon

His ocean-beaten mug— "
    "The Dutchman came undaunted to
the scratch,
But found the champion there already. Both
Most heartily shook hands, amid the cheers
Of their encouraged backers. Two to one
Was offered on the Melbourne nonpareil;
And soon, so fit the Flying Dutchman seemed,
Found takers everywhere. No time was lost
In getting to the business of the day.
The Dutchman led at once, and seemed to land
On Byron's dicebox; but the seaman's reach,
Too short for execution at long shots,
Did not get fairly home upon the ivory;
And Byron had the best of the exchange."
    "Round Three: the rumors that had
gone about
Of a breakdown in Byron's training
Seemed quite confirmed. Upon the call of time
He rose, and, looking anything but cheerful,
Proclaimed with every breath Bellows to Mend.
At this point six to one was freely offered
Upon the Dutchman; and Lord Worthington
Plunged at this figure till he stood to lose
A fortune should the Dutchman, as seemed certain,
Take down the number of the Panley boy.

The Dutchman, glutton as we know he is,
Seemed this time likely to go hungry. Cashel
Was clearly groggy as he slipped the sailor,
Who, not to be denied, followed him up,
Forcing the fighting mid tremendous cheers."

"Forty to one, the Dutchman's friends exclaimed.
Done, said Lord Worthington, who shewed himself
A sportsman every inch. Barely the bet
Was booked, when, at the reeling champion's jaw
The sailor, bent on winning out of hand,
Sent his right. The issue seemed a cert,
When Cashel, ducking smartly to his left,
Cross-countered like a hundredweight of brick— "

"A scene of indescribable excitement
Ensued; for it was now quite evident
That Byron's grogginess had all along
Been feigned to make the market of his backers.
We trust this sample of colonial smartness
Will not find imitators on this side.
The losers settled up like gentlemen;
But many thought that Byron shewed bad taste
In taking out old Ned Skene upon his back,
And, with Bob Mellish tucked beneath his oxter,
Sprinting a hundred yards to show the crowd
The perfect pink of his condition."

The Admirable Bashville; or, Constancy Unrewarded, Act II

Cetewayo, a man who has come to watch Cashel Byron's boxing match, rails against the British.

CETEWAYO

Have I been brought a million miles by sea
To learn how men can lie! Know, Father Weber,
Men become civilized through twin diseases,
Terror and Greed to wit: These two conjoined
Become the grisly parents of invention.
Why does the trembling white with frantic toil
Of hand and brain produce the magic gun
That slays a mile off, whilst the manly Zulu
Dares look his foe i' the face; fights foot to foot;
Lives in the present; drains the Here and Now;
Makes life a long reality, and death
A moment only; whilst your Englishman
Glares on his burning candle's winding-sheets,
Counting the steps of his approaching doom,
And in the murky corners ever sees
Two horrid shadows, Death and Poverty:
In the which anguish an unnatural edge
Comes on his frighted brain, which straight devises
Strange frauds by which to filch unearned gold,
Mad crafts by which to slay unfaced foes,

Until at last his agonized desire
Makes possibility its slave. And then—
Horrible climax! All-undoing spite!—
Th' importunate clutching of the coward's hand
From wearied Nature Devastation's secrets
Doth wrest; when straight the brave
black-livered man
Is blown explosively from the globe;
And Death and Dread, with their white-livered slaves,
Oer-run the earth, and through their chattering teeth
Stammer the words "Survival of the Fittest."
Enough of this: I came not here to talk.
Thou sayest thou hast two white-faced ones who dare
Fight without guns, and spearless, to the death.
Let them be brought.

The secret to being miserable is to have leisure to bother about whether you are happy or not.
G.B.S., *Misalliance,* Preface

How He Lied to Her Husband

Her Husband comes upon He and She as they are deciding the best way to continue their love affair.

HER HUSBAND

What is Mrs. Bompas to you, I'd like to know. I'll tell you what Mrs. Bompas is. She's the smartest woman in the smartest set in South Kensington, and the handsomest, and the cleverest, and the most fetching to experienced men who know a good thing when they see it, whatever she may be to conceited penny-a-lining puppies who think nothing good enough for them. It's admitted by the best people; and not to know it argues yourself unknown. Three of our actor-managers have offered her a hundred a week if she'll go on the stage when they start a repertory theatre; and I think they know what they're about as well as you. The only member of the present Cabinet that you might call a handsome man has neglected the business of the country to dance with her, though he don't belong to our set as a regular thing. One of the most professional poets in Bedford Park wrote a sonnet to her, worth all your amateur trash. At Ascot last season the eldest son of a duke excused himself from calling on me on the ground that his feelings for Mrs. Bompas were not consistent with his duty to me as a host; and it did him honor and me too.

But (*With gathering fury.*) she isn't good enough for you, it seems. You regard her with coldness, with indifference; and you have the cool cheek to tell me so to my face.

For two pins I'd flatten your nose in to teach you manners. Introducing a fine woman to you is casting pearls before swine (*Screaming at him.*) before SWINE! d'ye hear?

> *A lifetime of happiness! No man alive could bear it: It would be hell on earth.*
> G.B.S., *Man and Superman*

Arms and the Man, Act I

The Man (Bluntschli) has broken into Petkoff's house after deserting his regiment, and is attempting to explain his contempt for war to Raina.

MAN

There are only two sorts of soldiers: old ones and young ones. I've served fourteen years: half of your fellows never smelt powder before. Why, how is it that you've just beaten us? Sheer ignorance of the art of war, nothing else. (*Indignantly.*) I never saw anything so unprofessional. Is it professional to throw a regiment of cavalry on a battery of machine guns, with the dead certainty that if the guns go off not a horse or man will ever get within fifty yards of the fire? I couldn't believe my eyes when I saw it. It's a funny sight. It's like slinging a handful of peas against a window pane: First one comes; then two or three close behind him; and then all the rest are in a lump. That's what you'd have said if you'd seen the first man in the charge today. He did it like an operatic tenor—a regular handsome fellow, with flashing eyes and lovely moustache, shouting a war-cry and charging like Don Quixote at windmills. We nearly burst with laughter at him; but when the sergeant ran up as white as a sheet, and told us they'd sent us the wrong cartridges, and that we couldn't fire a shot for the next ten minutes, we laughed at the other side of our mouths. I never felt so sick in my life, though I've been in one or two very tight places. And I hadn't even a revolver cartridge—nothing but chocolate. We'd no bayonets—nothing. Of course, they just cut us to bits. And there was Don Quixote flourishing like a drum major, thinking he'd done the cleverest thing ever known, whereas he ought to be courtmartialled for it. Of all the fools ever let loose on the field of battle, that man must be the very maddest. He and his regiment simply committed suicide—only the pistol missed fire, that's all.

He knows nothing; and he thinks he knows everything. That points clearly to a political career.
G.B.S., *Major Barbara*

Arms and the Man, Act III

Nicola, one of the Petkoff's servants, is trying to woo Louka (the maid) back from Sergius.

NICOLA

(*With unwavering self-assertion.*) Who was it made you give up wearing a couple of pounds of false black hair and reddening your lips and cheeks like any other Bulgarian girl? I did. Who taught you to trim your nails, and keep your hands clean, and be dainty about yourself, like a fine Russian lady? Me! do you hear that? Me! I've often thought that if Raina were out of the way, and you just a little less of a fool and Sergius just a little more of one, you might come to be one of my grandest customers, instead of only being my wife and costing me money.

If you want to be a lady, your present behavior to me won't do at all, unless when we're alone. It's too sharp and impudent; and impudence is a sort of familiarity: it shews affection for me. And don't you try being high and mighty with me either.

You're like all country girls: you think it's genteel to treat a servant the way I treat a stable-boy. That's only your ignorance; and don't forget it. And don't be so ready to defy everybody. Act as if you expected to have your own way, not as if you expected to be ordered about.

The way to get on as a lady is the same as the way to get on as a servant: You've got to know your place; that's the secret of it. And you may depend on me to know my place if you get promoted. Think it over, my girl. I'll stand by you: One servant should always stand by another.

> *The English have no respect for their language, and will not teach their children to speak it. It is impossible for an Englishman to open his mouth, without making some other Englishman despise him.*
> G.B.S., *Pygmalion,* Preface

The Man of Destiny

In this speech, Napoleon is pontificating on the English.

NAPOLEON

No Englishman is too low to have scruples: No Englishman is high enough to be free from their tyranny. But every Englishman is born with a certain miraculous power that makes him master of the world. When he wants a thing, he never tells himself that he wants it. He waits patiently until there comes into his mind, no one knows how, a burning conviction that it his moral and religious duty to conquer those who have got the thing he wants. Then he becomes irresistible. Like the aristocrat, he does what pleases him and grabs what he wants: Like the shopkeeper, he pursues his purpose with the industry and steadfastness that come with strong religious conviction and deep sense of moral responsibility. He is never at loss for an effective moral attitude. As the great champion of freedom and national independence, he conquers and annexes half the world, and calls it Colonization. When he wants a new market for his adulterated Manchester goods, he sends a missionary to teach the natives the gospel of peace. The natives kill the missionary: he flies to arms in defence of Christianity; fights for it; conquers for it; and takes the market as a reward from heaven. In defence of his island shores, he puts a chaplain on board his ship; nails a flag with a cross on it to his top-gallant mast; and sails to the ends of the earth, sinking, burning, and destroying all who dispute the empire of the seas with him. He boasts that a slave is free the moment his foot touches British soil; and he sells the children of his poor at six years of age to work under the lash in his factories for sixteen hours a day. He makes two revolutions, and then declares war on our one in the name of law and order. There is nothing so bad or so good that you will not find Englishmen doing it; but you will never find an Englishman in the wrong. He does everything on principle. He fights you on patriotic principles; he robs you on business principles; he enslaves you on imperial principles; he bullies you on manly principles; he supports his king on loyal principles; and cuts off his king's head on republican principles. His watchword is always duty; and he never forgets that the nation which lets its duty get on the opposite side to its interest is lost.

He who can does. He who cannot, teaches.
G.B.S., *Man and Superman*

Widower's Houses, Act II

Lickcheese, the agent of Sartorius, a slum landlord, has just been fired for making necessary safety repairs in one of Sartorius' tenements.

LICKCHEESE

Mark my words, gentlemen: He'll find what a man he's lost the very first week's rents the new man'll bring him. You'll find the difference yourself, Dr. Trench, if you and your children come into the property. I have got money when no other collector alive would have wrung it out. And this is the thanks I get for it! Why, see here, gentlemen! Look at that bag of money on the table. Hardly a penny of that but there was a hungry child crying for the bread it would have bought. But I got it for him—screwed and worried and bullied it out of them. I—look here, gentlemen: I'm pretty well seasoned to the work; but there's money there that I couldn't have taken if it hadn't been for the thought of my own children depending on me for giving him satisfaction. And because I charged him four-and-twenty shillin' to mend a staircase that three women have been hurt on, and that would have got him prosecuted for manslaughter if it had been let go much longer, he gives me the sack. Wouldn't listen to a word, though I would have offered to make up the money out of my own pocket—aye, and am willing to do it still if you only put in a word for me, sir. I never heard him say he was satisfied yet—no, nor he wouldn't, not if I skinned 'em alive. I don't say he's the worst landlord in London: he couldn't be worse than some; but he's no better than the worst I ever had to do with. And, though I say it, I'm better than the best collector he ever done business with. I have screwed more and spent less on his properties than anyone would believe that knows what such properties are. I know my merits, Dr. Trench, and will speak for myself if no one else will.

Optimistic lies have such immense therapeutic value that a doctor who cannot tell them convincingly has mistaken his profession.
G.B.S., *Misalliance,* Preface

The Widower's Houses, Act II

Sartorius, a slum landlord, justifies his actions in relationship to the upkeep (or lack of it) of his tenements.

SARTORIUS

I am glad to find that so far we are in perfect sympathy. I am, of course, a Conservative; not a narrow or prejudiced one, I hope, nor at all opposed to true progress, but still a sound conservative. As to Lickcheese, I need say no more about him than that I have dismissed him from my service this morning for a breach of trust; and you will hardly accept his testimony as friendly or disinterested. As to my business, it is simply to provide homes suited to the small means of very poor people, who require roofs to shelter them just like other people. Do you suppose I can keep up these roofs for nothing!

You are welcome to replace all the missing banisters, handrails, cistern lids, and dust-hole tops at your own expense; and you will find them missing again in less than three days—burnt, sir, every stick of them. I do not blame the poor creatures: They need fires, and often have no other way of getting them. But I really cannot spend pound after pound in repairs for them to pull down, when I can barely get them to pay me four and sixpence a week for a room, which is the recognized fair London rent. No, gentlemen: When people are very poor, you cannot help them, no matter how much you may sympathize with them. It does them more harm than good in the long run. I prefer to save my money in order to provide additional houses for the homeless, and to lay by a little for Blanche.

When I, to use your own words, screw and bully, and drive these people to pay what they have freely undertaken to pay me, I cannot touch one penny of the money they give me until I have first paid you your £700 out of it. What Lickcheese did for me, I do for you. He and I are alike intermediaries: you are the principal. It is because of the risks I run through the poverty of tenants that you extract interest from me at the monstrous and exorbitant rate of seven percent, forcing me to extract the uttermost farthing in my turn from the tenants. And yet, Dr. Trench, you have not hesitated to speak contemptuously of me because I have applied my industry and forethought to the management of our property, and am maintaining it by the same honourable means.

> *Self-denial is not a virtue; it is only the effect of prudence on rascality.*
> G.B.S., *Man and Superman*

The Philanderer, Act I

Leonard Charteris, attempting to turn aside Julia's advances, reiterates the creed of the Ibsen Club, of with they are both members.

CHARTERIS

So it did, my dear. But that is not the point. As a woman of advanced years, you were determined to be free. You regarded marriage as a degrading bargain, by which a woman sold herself to a man for the social status of a wife and a right to be supported and pensioned in old age out of his income. That's the advanced view—our view. Besides, if you had married me, I might have turned out a drunkard, a criminal, an imbecile, a horror to you; and you couldn't have released yourself. Too big a risk, you see. That's the rational view—our view. Accordingly, you reserved the right to leave me at any time if you found our companionship incompatible with—what was the expression you used?—with your full development as a human being: I think that was how you put the Ibsenist view—our view. So I had to be content with a charming philander, which taught me a great deal, and brought me some hours of exquisite happiness.

I now assert the right I reserved—the right of breaking with you when I please. Advanced views, Julia, involve advanced duties: You cannot be an advanced woman when you want to bring a man to your feet, and a conventional woman when you want to hold him there against his will. Advanced people form charming friendships: Conventional people marry. Marriage suits a good deal of people: And its first duty is fidelity. Friendship suits some people; and its first duty is unhesitating, uncomplaining acceptance of a notice of a change of feeling from either side. You chose friendship instead of marriage. Now do your duty, accept your notice.

Do not love your neighbor as yourself. If you are on good terms with yourself it is an impertinence; if on bad, an injury.
G.B.S., *Man and Superman*

The Philanderer, Act III

After rejoicing that he was able to make medical history for discovering the cause of Colonel Craven's illness, Dr. Paramore finds out that there is really no such disease.

PARAMORE

It's natural of you to think only of yourself. I don't blame you: all invalids are selfish. It's the fault of the wickedly sentimental laws in this country. I was not able to make experiments enough—only three dogs and a monkey. Think of that—with all Europe full of my professional rivals—men burning to prove me wrong! There is freedom in France—enlightened republican France. One Frenchman experiments on two hundred monkeys to disprove my theory. Another sacrifices £36—three hundred dogs and three francs apiece—to upset the monkey experiments. A third proves them to be both wrong by a single experiment in which he lets the temperature of a camel's liver 60 degrees below zero. And now comes this cursed Italian who has ruined me. He has a government grant to buy animals with, besides the run of the largest hospital in Italy. But I won't be beaten by an Italian. I'll go to Italy myself. I'll rediscover my disease: I know it exists; I feel it; and I'll prove it if I have to experiment on every mortal animal that's got a liver at all.

Major Barbara, Act III

Barbara's father, Andrew Undershaft, the co-owner of a munitions factory, requires that a foundling be his heir and take over the plant. Barbara's fiance, Cusins, has decided to accept Undershaft's offer to adopt him, and justifies his decision in this monologue.

CUSINS

It is not the sale of my soul that troubles me: I have sold it too often to care about that. I have sold it for a professorship. I have sold it for an income. I have sold it to escape being imprisoned for refusing to pay taxes for hangman's ropes and unjust wars and things that I abhor. What is all human conduct but the daily and hourly sale of our souls for trifles? What I am now selling it for is neither money nor position nor comfort, but for reality and power.

I think all power is spiritual: These cannons will not go off by themselves. I have tried to make spiritual power by teaching Greek. But the world can never be really touched by a dead language and a dead civilization. The people must have power; and the people cannot have Greek.

You cannot have power for good without having power for evil too. Even mother's milk nourishes murderers as well as heroes. This power which only tears men's bodies to pieces has never been so horribly abused as the intellectual power, the imaginative power, the poetic, religious power that can enslave men's souls. As a teacher of Greek I gave the intellectual man weapons against the common man. I now want to give the common man weapons against the intellectual man. I love the common people. I want to arm them against the lawyers, the doctors, the priests, the literary men, the professors, the artists, and the politicians, who, once in authority, are more disastrous and tyrannical than all the fools, rascals, and impostors. I want a power simple enough for common men to use, yet strong enough to force the intellectual oligarchy to use its genius for the general good.

Man must master that power first. I admitted this when the Turks and Greeks were last at war. My best pupil went out to fight for Hellas. My parting gift to him was not a copy of Plato's *Republic,* but a revolver and a hundred Undershaft cartridges, The blood of every Turk he shot—if he shot any—is on my head as well as on Undershaft's. The act committed me to this place for ever. Your father's challenge has beaten me. Dare I make war on war? I dare. I must. I will.

Assassination is the extreme form of censorship.
G.B.S., "The Shewing-Up of Blanco Posnet," *The Limits of Toleration*

Major Barbara, Act III

In arguing his case to his son, Stephen, Undershaft belabors the hypocrisy that allows his business to thrive.

UNDERSHAFT

Oh, that's everybody's birthright. Look at poor little Jenny Hill, the Salvation lassie! she would think you were laughing at her if you asked her to stand up in the street and teach grammar or geography or mathematics or even drawing-room dancing; but it never occurs to her to doubt that she can teach morals and religion. You are all alike, you respectable people. You can't tell me the bursting strain of a ten-inch gun, which is a very simple matter; but you all think you can tell me the bursting strain of a man under temptation. You daren't handle high explosives; but you're all ready to handle honesty and truth and justice and the whole duty of man, and kill one another at that game. What a country! What a world! The government of your country! I am the government of your country: I, and Lazarus. Do you suppose that you and half a dozen amateurs like you, sitting in a row in that foolish gabble shop, can govern Undershaft and Lazarus? No, my friend: You will do what pays us. You will make war when it suits us, and peace when it doesn't. You will find out that trade requires certain measures when we have decided on those measures. When I want anything to keep my dividends up, you will discover that my want is a national need. When other people want something to keep my dividends down, you will call out the police and military. And in turn you shall have the support and applause of newspapers, and the delight of imagining that you are a great statesman. Government of your country! Be off with you, my boy, and play with your caucuses and leading articles and historic parties and great leaders and burning questions and the rest of your toys. I am going back to my counting-house to pay the piper and call the tune.

> *People are always blaming their circumstances for what they are. I don't believe in circumstances. The people who get on in this world are the people who get up and look at the circumstances they want, and, if they can't find them, make them.*
> G.B.S., *Mrs. Warren's Profession*

Caesar and Cleopatra, Act I

This monologue if from a scene at the beginning of the play. The Man is Caesar, contemplating the mystery and power of the Sphinx.

THE MAN

Hail, Sphinx, salutation from Julius Caesar! I have wandered in many lands, seeking the lost regions from which my birth into this world exiled me, and the company of creatures such as myself. I have found flocks and pastures, men and cities, but no other Caesar, no air native to me, no man kindred to me, none who can do my day's deed, and think my night's thought. In the little world yonder, Sphinx, my place is a high as yours in this great desert; only I wander, and you sit still; I conquer, and you endure, I work and wonder, and you watch and wait; I look up and am dazzled, look down and am darkened, look round and am puzzled, whilst your eyes never turn from looking out—out of the world—to the lost region—the home from which we have strayed. Sphinx, you and I, strangers to the race of men, are no strangers to one another: Have I not been conscious of you and of this place since I was born? Rome is a madman's dream: this is my Reality. These starry lamps of yours I have seen from afar in Gaul, in Britain, in Spain, in Thessaly, signalling great secrets to some eternal sentinel below, whose post I never could find. And here at last is their sentinel—an image of the constant and immortal part of my life, silent, full of thoughts, alone in the silver desert. Sphinx, Sphinx: I have climbed mountains at night to hear in the distance the stealthy footfalls of the winds that chase your sands in forbidden play—our invisible children. O Sphinx, laughing in whispers. My way hither was the way of destiny; for I am he of whose genius you are the symbol: Part brute, part woman, and part god—nothing of man in me at all. Have I read your riddle, Sphinx?

> *When two people are under the influence of the most violent, most insane, most delusive, and most transient of passions, they are required to swear that they will remain in that excited abnormal, and exhausting condition continuously until death do them part.*
> G.B.S., *Getting Married*

Candida, Act I

Marchbanks, the poet, has confessed his love for Morell's wife, Candida, to Morell.

MARCHBANKS

(*With petulant vehemence.*) Yes, it does. (*Morell turns away contemptuously. Marchbanks scrambles to his feet and follows him.*) You think because I shrink from being brutally handled—because (*With tears in his voice.*) I can do nothing but cry with rage when I am met with violence—because I can't lift a heavy trunk down from the top of a cab like you—because I can't fight you for your wife as a navvy would: All that makes you think I'm afraid of you. But you're wrong. If I haven't got what you call British pluck, I haven't got British cowardice either: I'm not afraid of a clergyman's ideas. I'll fight your ideas. I'll rescue her from her slavery to them. You are driving me out of the house because you daren't let her choose between your ideas and mine. You are afraid to let me see her again.

If you give any explanation but the true one, you are a liar and a coward. Tell her what I said; and how you were strong and manly, and shook me as a terrier shakes a rat; and how I shrank and was terrified; and how you called me a snivelling little whelp and put me out of the house. If you don't tell her, I will: I'll write it to her.

Candida, Act I

Morell tries to explain to Marchbanks why a relationship, illicit or otherwise, could never exist between Marchbanks and Morell's wife, Candida.

MORELL

(*He speaks with noble tenderness.*) Eugene: Listen to me. Some day, I hope and trust, you will be a happy man like me. You will be married; and you will be working with all your might and valor to make every spot on earth as happy as your own home. You will be one of the makers of the Kingdom of Heaven on earth; and—who knows?—you may be a pioneer and master builder where I am only a humble journeyman; for don't think, my boy, that I cannot see in you, young as you are, a promise of higher powers than I can ever pretend to. I well know that it is in the poet that the holy spirit of man—the god within him—is most godlike. It should make you tremble to think of that—to think that the heavy burthen and great gift of a poet may be laid upon you.

In the future—when you are as happy a I am—I will be your true brother in the faith. I will help you to believe that God has given us a world that nothing but our own folly keeps from being a paradise. I will help you to believe that your wife loves you and is happy in her home.

We need such help, Marchbanks: We need it greatly and always. There are so many things to make us doubt, if once we let our understanding be troubled. Even at home, we sit as if in a camp, encompassed by the hostile army of doubts. Will you play the traitor and let them in on me?

This is the true joy in life, the being used for a purpose recognized by yourself as a mighty one; the being thoroughly worn out before you are thrown on the scrap heap; the being a force of Nature instead of a feverish selfish little clod of ailments and grievances complaining that the world will not devote itself to making you happy.
G.B.S., *Man and Superman*